Spending the Night on the Pike

CreateSpace Independent Publishing Platform (2013; revised 2016)

ISBN-13: 1482771543
ISBN-10: 978-1482771541

Copyright Tim O'Gorman

Spending the Night on the Pike

A Postcard History of Motels Along US Highway 1
From Richmond to Petersburg 1920-1975

Tim O'Gorman

Acknowledgements & Credits

I am grateful for the help and support provided by friends and family during this project. Among those are Betty Bishop, a fellow co-worker, who took an interest early on in the postcard collection that I had accumulated and suggested that a book be written, and Joel and Susan Byrne, neighbors and friends whose willingness to proof my drafts and whose constant encouragement kept me going. Mike Uzel, an experienced post card collector, provided invaluable information on local history as well as the loan of postcards to supplement those in my collection that further illustrate the history of motels along US Highway 1. David Malgee, local historian, provided information on locations of motels no longer standing. My brother James, an experienced author, lent his editorial talents to early drafts along with enthusiastic support. And my family who, rather than being bemused and amused by my strange fascination with motels, kept me from being discouraged when challenges arose.

All postcard images and images of pamphlets and motel guides, are from my collection except where indicated. Other postcard images were obtained from the Chesterfield County Historical Society and from the postcard collection of Mr. Mike Uzel. Other images were obtained from the Library of Congress and the Virginia Department of Historic Resources. All contemporary images were taken by the author. Image sources are credited when used.

Preface

This book was inspired by a postcard, a postcard of a tourist court that I had noticed shortly after moving to Chester 20 years ago, one that I passed everyday on my way to work along Jefferson Davis Highway. It took me back to the family trips I had taken as a kid and of the thrill of spending the night in new and different places, an experience that always made the trip all that more adventurous. The tourist court, a relic of a bygone era, was well-preserved and still being used, although not as a motel. When I found the postcard, I discovered that I had also found an interest. Thus began 15 years of collecting postcards of motels along Highway 1 between Richmond and Petersburg , a pastime that has come to include the entire stretch of U.S. Highway 1 in Virginia.

Early tourist court entrepreneurs were advised by business start-up guides to use postcards as a way to advertise. Postcards were hugely popular in the early 20th century and motels gave them away free up through the 1970's. Not all of them did, however. As a result, this is not a complete catalog of all the tourist courts and motels that have existed along Highway 1 between Richmond and Petersburg, only those that published postcards that I've collected or borrowed. Also included in the narrative are images of surviving tourist courts for which I do not have contemporary postcards. Chapters are organized chronologically according to building types, beginning with camps and cottage courts, tourist homes, and motor courts, all of which are building styles that came to define motel architecture that changed over time.

U.S. Highway 1 was designated a National Highway in 1926, traversing from the Canadian border at Ft. Kent, Maine and by 1938, to Key West, Florida. The highway entered the Commonwealth at Alexandria, passing through Fredericksburg, Richmond, and Petersburg before reaching South Hill. Until the arrival of the interstates it was the most heavily traveled highway in Virginia. From Henrico County to Dinwiddie County, Highway 1 has had a variety of local names throughout its history; Richmond-Petersburg Turnpike, Brook Road, Washington Highway, Jefferson Davis Highway, the Boulevard, and Boydton Plank Road. These street names are used when providing addresses and locations, and the motels are listed in order north to south as tourists driving to Florida would have encountered them.

The motels along the four-lane Richmond-Petersburg Turnpike built in 1958, later to become a part of Interstate 95, are also addressed. While their appearance marked the end of the Highway 1 motel heyday many of those, too, were later to close because of competition and economic downturns or were to lose their franchise affiliations and become owned by local corporations. And while the focus is on Highway 1, the stretch of U.S. Highway 301 that branched off at Petersburg is included because of that highway's popularity with travelers and the number of motels that once thrived along South Crater Road.

Finding where the old tourist courts and motels were located was achieved by "roadside archaeology", driving the highways and searching. For those motels still in operation, the task was easy but for those no longer in existence some detective work was required. Vintage topographical maps and historical aerial photographs available online from the United State Geological Survey and Google Earth were used to assist in verifying locations as was anecdotal information gleaned from published sources. When the exact location of a motel is uncertain, the approximate vicinity to other landmarks is provided.

This book is not a history of postcards. It is a history of what postcards tell us about travelers in the first half of the 20th century and of the evolution of the lodging that accommodated them. For many tourist courts and motels, postcards are the only record remaining of these once vibrant businesses and are the source of clues that help identify buildings that still remain but are hidden or disguised. For those motels still operating, their postcards give us a glimpse of their former glory, when they were new and polished, before the arrival of the interstates that siphoned off the tourist business. And they tell of the time when motels were family-owned "Mom and Pop's" and proudly advertised that fact on their postcards. It is also a nostalgic look back for those who remember the time when road trips required driving through towns instead of around them and of a time that seems less complicated, less stressful, and less rushed. And for those who take the time to look, the motels, tourist courts, and tourist cabins still standing provide us a reminder of that earlier time.

The postcard that inspired the book – Andrews Modern Cottages, ca. 1945. Andrews is located at 17100 Jefferson Davis Highway and is currently the home of The Shops At Ivey. Details of this cottage court can be found in Chapter 1.

Contents

Chapter 1 - Prologue 1

Chapter 2- Camps, Cabins, Inns, and Cottage Courts – 1920 to 1950 3

Chapter 3 - Camps of Crime – Camps of Quality 44

Chapter 4 - Tourist Homes – 1920-1950 47

Chapter 5 - Motor Courts, Auto Courts, Tourist Courts, and Motels – 1940 to 1970 69

Chapter 6 - The Green Book. 92

Chapter 7 - Interstates and Motel Chains – 1950 to 1975 95

Chapter 8 - U.S. Highway 301 – Petersburg Motels 109

Chapter 9 - Epilog 122

Chapter Endnotes 124

Bibliography 127

Chapter 1

Prologue

America's life-long love affair with the automobile happened overnight. In 1893 the Duryea brothers demonstrated that a gasoline engine could power a vehicle; by 1910 there were over 469,000 vehicles Nationwide, 2,700 in Virginia alone.[1] In 1895, only two years after the Duryea's breakthrough, the American Motor League was established to promote better roads and in 1902 the American Automobile Association was founded.[2] By 1920 the number of vehicles owned by Americans had grown to over 9.2 million due to the proliferation of auto makers and to the innovations of Henry Ford whose production line method pioneered in 1903 produced vehicles more quickly.

(Library of Congress Image)

The automobile industry spawned complementary services; business opportunities for entrepreneurs to own and operate gasoline stations, open roadside eateries, publish guide books, sell automotive accessories, and provide lodging for motorized travelers and tourists. This lodging, which came to be called motels, was developed specifically to meet a demand that hotels could not satisfy. Hotels were most often located within cities and towns close to the railroads, did not provide parking, did not welcome dirty, road weary travelers, and did not provide the experience that road adventurers were seeking. Americans had quickly developed a passion for the freedom that automobiles provided. No longer bound by the dictates of railroads with their set routes and timetables, travelers could now determine their own destinations and travel at their own pace. The primitive roads of the early 20th century, along with mechanical breakdowns these early automobiles often experienced, only added to the adventure. For those who chose not to stay in hotels, auto camping became the method to overnight while traveling. Travelers camped along the side of a road, a practice that, as the pastime grew more popular, caused friction with local landowners who resented these "tin can tourists" and the trash they left behind. To control the ever- increasing numbers of travelers while at the same time coveting tourist dollars, some municipalities built campgrounds for motorists, charging a fee for amenities, while some landowners opened private campgrounds as business ventures.

Auto camping in Yellowstone Park, ca. 1923
(Library of Congress Image)

Hotels and auto camping were the choices throughout the 1910's, but as the number of motorists grew and as tastes and preferences changed, campground owners learned that the public was willing to pay for added conveniences such as cabins, garages, running water, and heat. Tourist cabins and cottages began to appear in increasing numbers creating competition that in turn led to even more amenities being offered. Soon establishments began providing restaurants, gift shops, private garages, gasoline, and car repair services.

By the 1930's, tourist lodgings were well established and had become a vibrant industry, competing with hotels that up to that time had looked upon these roadside cottage camps with disdain. In Central Virginia, the number of tourist courts had become so numerous that the editor of the *Richmond News Leader* noted most of the tourist establishments were not prospering because of over building.[3] By 1940, there were 54 registered tourist lodgings in Chesterfield County and another 37 in Henrico, most of which were located along U.S. Highway 1.[4]

As the tourist lodging industry matured along with the automobile, building styles evolved from what was initially clusters of cabins and cottages arranged in no specific manner to more symmetrical arrangements. Later, cabins became adjoined in court yard-style layouts and then to one-story buildings divided into rooms laid out in "L's" or "U's", designed to facilitate guests being able to park at their room door. They also adopted a variety of names such as cottage courts, tourist courts, auto courts, motor courts, motor lodges, and motels, a blending of the words of "motor" and "hotel".

Along U.S. Highway 1 stretching from the north of Richmond in Henrico County to the south of Petersburg in Dinwiddie County, the history of automobile traveling, and the lodgings that accommodated them, can be traced by the early motels and tourist courts that still remain and, for those who look closely, are hidden. Time and progress have erased many of them. Of those that remain, some continue to cater to travelers and transients, some have become "extended stay" apartments, some have been transformed into other businesses, some are relics or ruins, and some are disguised. Together they represent the early age of automobile travel in Central Virginia and of the time before Interstate 95 when U.S. Highway 1 was "America's Main Street".

U.S. Highway 1 Construction 1930
(Library of Congress Image)

Chapter 2

Camps, Cabins, Inns, and Cottage Courts – 1920 to 1950

The attraction of the open road and the adventure that it promised gave rise to auto camping - finding a place to stop, pitching a tent, cooking over an open fire, and moving on to repeat the experience. Local entrepreneurs began operating campgrounds to control unwanted camping on private property. Offering few amenities at first, some campground owners began constructing cabins for those unwilling, or too tired, to pitch tents. These cabins were crudely built, and unheated with bare furnishings. If mattresses were needed, travelers would pay extra.

The demand for lodging continued to increase as more Americans began to travel and landowners whose lands bordered highways found that building and operating camps was a profitable business. By 1933, there were over 30,000 cabin camps throughout the United States, cabin camps being one of the few booming businesses during the Depression.[1]

As time went on camp owners learned that tourists were willing to pay for comfort and amenities and began to build cabins with better, longer lasting materials, heat, running water, showers and baths, and other comforts one would expect in their own home. To distinguish these improved cabins from the previous ones, and to alert travelers of these amenities, the term "cottage" came into use. By 1930, the term "court" was added to describe the layout of the motel; cottages arranged around a central area or courtyard.

The terms motel, cottages, tourist court, cabins, motor court, etc. were used interchangeably, all meaning the same. The following examples of cottage courts are the earliest motels in the area that were arranged as individual cottages and varied patterns. They sometimes offered restaurants, or other services including gas stations and grocery stores. Some establishments enjoyed a long success and evolved from cabin camps, to courts, to motels in architectural styles; some are still in business.

1940 American Motel Association Guide

1937 United Courts Guide

1940's Highway 1 Guide

Henrico County –
North to South on Highway 1
(Brook Road)

The Ninan

In business from the 1930's until 1974, the Ninan was constructed as cottages adjoined, an architectural style that would later be called motor court. It was also designed with a southwestern theme, a style that was popular in the east but one of the only examples in this area. The Ninan, located at 1204 Old Francis Road and the intersection with Highway 1, was demolished in the 1970's.

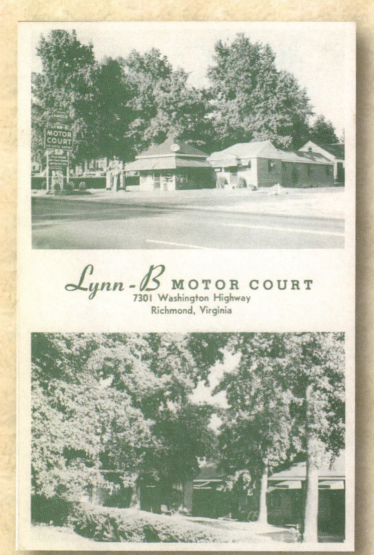

Lynn-B Motor Court

The Lynn-B Motor Court was built in 1937 in the cottage court style. It featured steam heated brick cottages, air conditioning, private tile baths, television, and kitchenettes. It also advertised its proximity to golfing, swimming, horseback riding, and theaters. Located at 7301 Brook Road, the Lynn-B went out of business about 1974 but remnants of this motor court remain; the former motel office is currently a fast food restaurant, "Sam's Burgers and Subs".

2012 View

Park Motel & Cottages

The Park Motel was built in the 1940's and was located at 7220 Brook Road at the intersection with Lakeside Drive. The Park offered travelers a choice of 21 private cottages or hotel rooms on "beautifully landscaped grounds all with private tiled baths." Today nothing remains of the Park. Its site is currently occupied by a car wash.

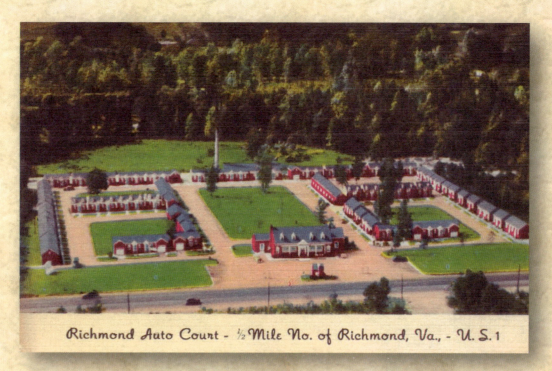

Richmond Auto Court

The Richmond Auto Court was one of the largest and most elaborately designed cottage courts in the area. Arranged as cottages adjoined, each unit had a separate garage and represents an early example of the transition from the cottage court to the motor court style of motel architecture. The amenities included auto services, an adjoining 18-hole golf course, and a restaurant, once considered an excellent place to eat for travelers and local residents alike. The Richmond Auto Court was located at 7204 Brook Road, now the site of The Dump discount furniture store.

Royall's Tourist Camp & Cottages

Royall's Tourist Camp was located at 5419 Brook Road. Offering both camping and cottages, Royall's advertised it's showers, camp supplies and accessories, and exhorted travelers to "stop a while and make yourself at home." The 1929 and 1935 Richmond Telephone Directories listed, in addition to Royall's, Bowman's New Tourist Camp, Breedlove Tourist Camp, Fireside Tourist Camp, and R.J. Hall's Tourist Camp, all located north of Richmond along Highway 1. No evidence of these early camps remain. The postcard above, postmarked 1927, contains the note, "We stopped here on our way up."

Henrico Auto Court/Colonial Court Motel

The Henrico Auto Court was located at 5207 Brook Road. Built in the early 1940's, the property was renamed the Colonial Hotel Court in the 1950's and later took the name Colonial Court Motel. It was built in the cottage court style with double cottages with a homey appearance to attract tourists. The Henrico Auto Court advertised itself as a "New 100 per cent modern court", only ½ block from a Howard Johnson's Restaurant, and a "Safe Place for Lady Tourists." The site of this auto court is now a vacant lot.

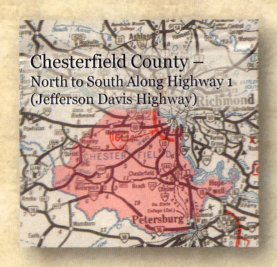

Chesterfield County –
North to South Along Highway 1
(Jefferson Davis Highway)

Grantham's Inn

Travelers who sent this postcard home in 1938 noted that they "….Have a nice double cabin. Hot water, steam heat and we needed it, etc." Grantham's Inn was located at 7301 Jefferson Davis but is no longer standing. Some owners used the term "inn" to attract travelers looking for the atmosphere that the word inn implied.

Fort Darling Motel

The Fort Darling Motel was built in 1957, one of the last cottage courts built in Chesterfield County. It advertised "Cosy o'night and vacation units, with family accommodations. Restaurants close by." Located at 7511 Jefferson Davis Highway, this establishment is still standing and continues to do business as the "Family Motel".

2012 View

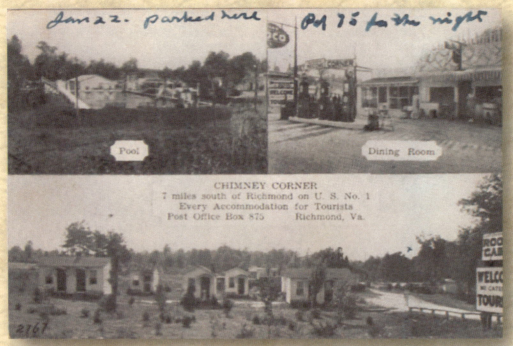

Chimney Corner

The Chimney Corner, located at 8610 Jefferson Davis Highway is one of the oldest motorists' establishments in Chesterfield County.[2] The Chimney Corner offered it all; modern cottages, a dining room, trailer space, rooms in a private home, private baths, gasoline station, and shaded lawns. The last remains of this tourist court was demolished in 2104.

2012 View

Bellwood Manor Motel

Built in the late 1940's, Bellwood Manor was constructed as a cottage court with double cottages arranged in a U-shape. Located just north of the intersection of Willis Road in the vicinity of the 9100 block of Jefferson Davis Highway, the Bellwood was demolished in the 1980's.

1979 View (Virginia Department of Historic Resources)

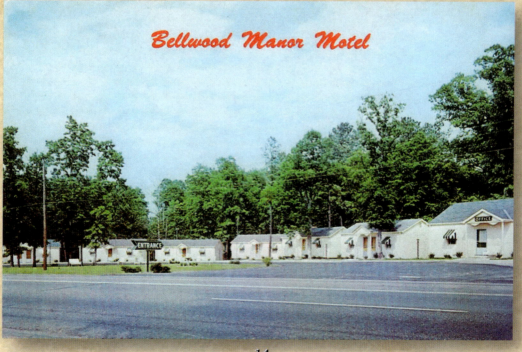

Oak Grove Tourist Court / Ford's Motor Court

1979 View
(Virginia Department of Historic Resources)

"These are lovely cabins" wrote one 1950's traveler of Ford's Motor Court. Called Oak Grove beginning in 1950, it was later renamed after the owners, the T.R. Ford family. Located at the intersection of Egee Drive in the vicinity of the 9800 block of Jefferson Davis Highway, this tourist court survived until the late 1970's before being demolished.

Kirkman's Tourist Court/Motel

Dating from the late 1930's, Kirkman's Tourist Court was initially designed in the cottage court style. It was later remodeled as adjoining cottages and renamed Kirkman's Motel. Located at 10321 Jefferson Davis Highway, the main portion of this motel is still standing and is currently occupied by Star Auto Sales.

2012 View

KIRKMAN'S MOTEL - Half way between Richmond and Petersburg, Virginia on U. S. Route No. 1

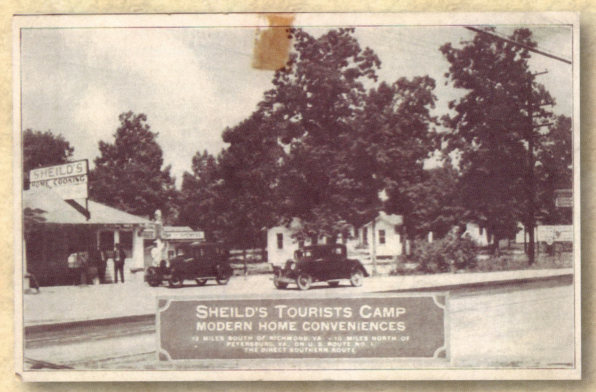

Sheild's Tourists Camp

Sheild's Tourists Camp was located at 11648 Jefferson Davis Highway at the intersection of Osborne Road. Dating from the 1930's, it is an example of an early cabin camp that offered shelter along with "Home Cooking". Sheild's later became Parnell's Tourist Court.

The Virginia Inn

An example of a traditional roadside inn, the Virginia Inn was located at the Osborne Road and Jefferson Davis Highway intersection. It was later renamed the Dutch Gap Inn and remained in business into the 1940's. It advertised rooms for tourists, meals and sandwiches, and "certerifed" water. The inn is no longer standing. (Chesterfield County Historical Society image)

Parnell's Tourist Court

Parnell's was located at 11648 Jefferson Davis Highway, the former Sheild's Tourists Camp at the intersection with Osborne Road, and advertised …."Every Cottage with Bath, Steam Heat, Inner-spring Mattress and Television." The restaurant offered "…Broiled Steaks, Southern Fried Chicken and Seafood." By the 1950's motels were including television as an amenity. Parnell's was demolished in the early 1970's. The property is now the site of a former 7-Eleven convenience store.

Goyne's Auto Camp/Dutch Gap Camp

Originally called Goyne's after its owner, Dutch Gap Camp was located at the southeast corner of the intersection of Jefferson Davis Highway and Osborne Road. This postcard dates from between 1923 and 1926 before Virginia State Route 31 was re-numbered as U.S. Highway 1. Privately owned, the Dutch Gap Camp was perhaps the first auto camp in Chesterfield County. [4] The auto camp offered cabins as well as tent space.

This photograph inspired a postcard. This image of Goyne's Auto Camp was colorized for the above postcard to include adding flowers to the foreground. (Chesterfield County Historical Society image)

Dutch Gap Tourist Court

"Motor Court: Dutch Gap. 35 guests are well taken care of in pleasant brick cottages, finished with knotty pine, and furnished in maple. All rms. WB." – from the 1946 edition of Duncan Hines' *Lodging for the Night*.[5] The Dutch Gap Tourist Court was located in the 11700 block of Jefferson Davis Highway at the southeast intersection with Osborne Road. By the 1960's the cottages were being rented as apartments and the grounds included trailer parks. The tourist court was demolished in 2003 and is now the site of a Wawa convenience store.

1979 View (Virginia Department of Historic Resources)

Robert E. Lee Court

The Robert E. Lee Court was designed in a unique manner with distinctively styled buildings. Built in 1949, the Robert E. Lee Court was located at 11716 Jefferson Davis Highway. Historic site surveyors in 1979 noted that the Robert E. Lee was the most "pleasant and imaginative grouping employed by any motel in Chesterfield." [6] The establishment promoted its four room colonial styled suites and its convenience to historic sites. The Robert E. Lee Court was demolished in the early 1980's.

1979 View
(Virginia Department of Historic Resources)

Lee's Tourist Court

Built in 1938, Lee's Tourist Court is located at 13501 Jefferson Davis Highway. Lee's offered 21 cottage units along with a dining room for guests. The establishment is currently the #1 General Store along with other small businesses. No postcard of this tourist court has been located.

2012 Views

Casey's Tourist Cottages

Casey's Tourist Cottages advertised its steam-heated cabins, private baths, and inner-spring mattresses. This card is postmarked April 1941, and was sent by tourists who had just visited Washington D.C. to see the cherry blossoms. Remnants of Casey's are still standing as the Roadrunner Quick Stop and trailer park located at 13900 Jefferson Davis Highway.

2012 View

Up-Away Guest Home & Cottages

Called the "Min-wah-yak" (place of rest) in the late 1930's, the Up-Away Guest Home was a tourist home that also offered cottages. On this postcard dated 1951, travelers wrote that they had driven from Cornwall, New York, a 400 mile, 10 hour trip, and intended to spend a week at the Up-Away. This establishment is still intact at 15300 Jefferson Davis Highway .

2012 View

Pine Acres Cottages

The Pine Acres Cottages was located near the intersection of Jefferson Davis Highway and Happy Hill Road. "PINE ACRES COTTAGES. On U.S. 1, 301, 16 miles south of Richmond, 5 miles north of Petersburg. Modern granite and brick cottages, back from road, steam heat, Private bath, tub and shower in each cottage. Mrs. Frank Bassett, Owner-Operator. Phone Petersburg 185W3." - from the 1950 *Virginia Tourist Association Guide*.[9] Pine Acres was demolished in the 1980's.

1979 View
(Virginia Department of Historic Resources)

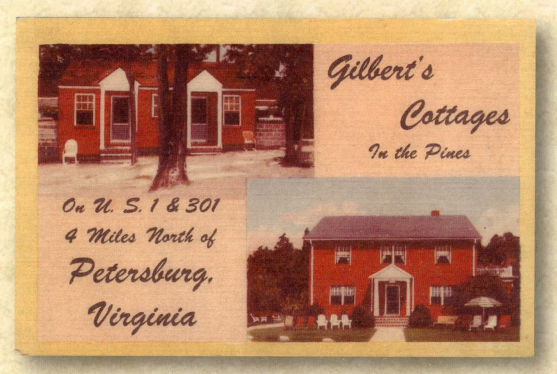

Gilbert's Cottages

Built in 1945, Gilbert's cottages most likely began as a tourist home. Most of the pines are gone but Gilbert's structures remain. Gilbert's advertised its Beautyrest inner-spring mattresses as one of its amenities. Mass production of inner-spring mattresses did not occur until 1925 and thus were not readily available to the average consumer at this time so motel owners promoted their Beautyrest mattresses as an added enticement to travelers. Gilbert's is still intact at 16413 Jefferson Davis Highway.

2012 View

Danner's Motor Court

"DANNER'S MOTOR COURT and Restaurant. Homemade candies, fountain service, gift shoppe, modern cottages with electric radiant heat, private baths. On U.S. 1 and 301, 16 miles south of Richmond. Mrs. Lucille M. Danner, owner-manager. RFD 3, Petersburg, Va." - from the 1950 *Virginia Tourist Court Guide*.[10] Danner's was built in 1950 and was constructed as individual cottages along with a restaurant. Located at 16601 Jefferson Davis Highway, the restaurant stayed in business through the 1970's and is currently Mary's This and That store.

2012 View

1979 View
(Virginia Department of Historic Resources)

Russell's Cottages

Built in the 1930's, Russell's Cottages advertised "Modern Heated Cottages with private baths" along with a dining room and gift shop. Vacant buildings are all that remain of this establishment located at 16701 Jefferson Davis Highway.

2012 View

Oak View Tourist Court/Motel

The Oak View Tourist Court was built in the late 1930's in the cottage court style featuring modern brick cottages with showers and Beautyrest mattresses. In 1956 the Oak View was renovated and updated to a more modern motel style of construction. Located at 16800 Jefferson Davis Highway, the motel was later renamed the Par 3 Motel.

2012 View

Shamrock Cottages

The Shamrock Motel, located at 16930 Jefferson Davis Highway, was built in 1948 in the cottage court style. The 1950 *Virginia Tourist Court Guide* had a listing for the Shamrock: "SHAMROCK COTTAGES. 3 ½ miles north of Petersburg, 18 miles south of Richmond on U.S. 1 and 301. Modern brick cottages, private baths, steam heat, radios. Television. Mrs. Glennis Jones. Phone Petersburg 5192J2. R.F.D. No. 3, Box 176, Petersburg, Va."[11] The motel is still in use as apartments. No postcard has been located for these cottages.

Andrews Modern Cottages

Andrews Modern Cottages offered "Automatic Hot Water Heat" and advertised that they had "State Board of Health Approved Water". They also promoted their "best equipment" and furniture along with Beautyrest box springs and mattresses. Andrews Modern Cottages is located at 17100 Jefferson Davis Highway near the intersection of Harrowgate Road, and is one of the best preserved examples of an early cottage court along Highway 1. It has remained unchanged since the 1930's and is currently the home of "The Shops At Ivey".

1979 View
(Virginia Department of Historic Resources)

2012 View

The Van Dyke Lodge, on U. S. 1, 4 miles north of Petersburg, Va.

Van Dyke Lodge

The term "lodge" was sometimes used by owners who wanted to make their cottages sound even more impressive to travelers. The Van Dyke Lodge offered hotel-type accommodations as well as cottages with private baths. No longer standing, the Van Dyke was located at 17113 Jefferson Davis Highway, currently the site of St Ann's Catholic Church.

Colonial Heights -
North to South Along Highway 1
(The Boulevard)

Matoaka Manor

"MATOAKA MANOR – TOURIST COURT. Petersburg, Va. Telephone 5521. Guest House-Brick Cottages. On U.S. Highway 1 and 301, 15 miles south of Richmond. John M. Ashby, Owner-Operator." - from the 1950 *Virginia Tourist Court Guide*.[12] Matoaka Manor offered hotel rooms along with cottages, breakfast included. This building still stands at 3597 Boulevard in Colonial Heights.

2012 View

Pickwick Lodge

"Guest House: Pickwick Lodge. 649 Blvd. One of those places you remember pleasantly long after you have said 'Good-bye'. 4 acres of ground, 8 rms, 9 cottages all WB. E. 2 WB $3.00-$5.00" – from the 1946 edition of Duncan Hines *Lodging for Night*. [13] Now demolished, the Pickwick Lodge was located on the Boulevard between Pickwick and Lynchburg Avenues. This is another example of a private home that offered cottages among its lodging options.

Northern Dinwiddie County –
North to South Along Highway 1
(Boydton Plank Road)

Ye Blue Tartane

Ye Blue Tartane located at 6620 Boydton Plank Road, south of Petersburg offered travelers brick cabins and modern tourist rooms, hot water heating, fans, a service station, restaurant, and a craft shop. Built in the 1930's, a portion of this cottage court still remains, operating as an antique shop.

YE BLUE TARTANE, ON U. S. HIGHWAY NO. 1, FIVE MILES SOUTH OF PETERSBURG, VIRGINIA

YE BLUE TARTANE, ON U. S. HIGHWAY NO. 1, 5 MILES SOUTH OF PETERSBURG, VIRGINIA

2012 View

Green Acres Court

The Green Acres Court offered cabins and later improved cottages with private baths, air conditioning (or window fans), free TV, and dining for guests. By the 1960's, Green Acres was advertising its location as 4 miles south of the then recently completed Richmond-Petersburg Turnpike Exit 1, today's I-85 exit 63. Little remains of the original Green Acres, now the site of a trailer park.

Chapter 3

Camps of Crime – Camps of Quality

Richmond News Leader, January 4, 1940

The unregulated nature of motels in the 1920's and '30's raised concerns from law enforcement officials about criminals making use of tourist courts as hideouts and for other illegal purposes. J. Edgar Hoover, in an article entitled "Camps of Crime" in the February 1940 issue of the *American Magazine*, made the case that tourist courts had become the home of "...disease, bribery, corruption, crookedness, rape, white slavery, thievery and murder..." and directed that police "'KEEP CLOSE WATCH ON TOURISTCAMPS!"[1]

Virginia officials were even more concerned about immoral activities conducted at tourist courts. In December 1939, the *Richmond News Leader* ran a series of investigative reports on conditions at local tourist camps and reported that in too many instances there was no attempt to register guests or to record license numbers and of the nine tourist courts investigated, most either condoned or ignored couples who were renting cabins and who were obviously not tourists. This was further confirmed when the reporter noticed several vehicles with local license plates and concluded that tourist camps were being used for romantic interludes by unmarried local couples.[2] By way of introducing the reports, editors of the newspaper noted that there was "...a clear distinction...between the road camps that are decent and legitimate and those that are nothing more than assignation houses." The editor called for legislation to better regulate tourist camps asking, "How shall this be done? What legislation should be enacted at the coming session of Assembly? The welfare of youth in Virginia demand an intelligent answer to those questions."[3]

Richmond News Leader, July 22, 1948

All these concerns, and the incidents that occurred, gave tourist courts a bad reputation or, as they came to be called, "no tell motels." Even those establishments that were legitimate and well-run were lumped together in the public's mind with those that were not. Legislation passed in February 1940 required Virginia tourist courts to register guests by name and to record license plate numbers that would be available for review by the police. Failure to do so would result in fines and jail time. It also directed that the tourist courts be kept clean and open for health inspectors and that a permit was required to operate as a tourist court, tourist home, or hotel. [4] The "Tourist Camp Bill" took effect in June 1940 and would, according to the editors of the *News Leader*, "...put camps out of business...but it will work toward a better and more comfortable camp at which the tired visitor may loll in the evening." [5]

The ease of anonymity offered by motels would continue to attract unlawful elements. But improving the appearance, quality, service, cleanliness, and safety of motels was not only the intent of legislators and local officials but of the motel owners themselves. By 1933, tourist court owners nation-wide realized the importance of organizing to promote their industry and to adopt industry standards. Hotels had been organized since 1910 by the American Hotel Association (AHA) but in 1933 the National Tourist Lodge and Motor Court Trade Association, later renamed International Motor Court Association, was launched as an industry organization for tourist courts and homes. In 1936 the American Motel Association was established with a focus on motels along tourist routes from New York to Florida. Members posted the Association logo on their advertising to let customers know that the motel was clean, had reasonable rates, and had high standards of service. [6]

Richmond News Leader, June 5, 1950

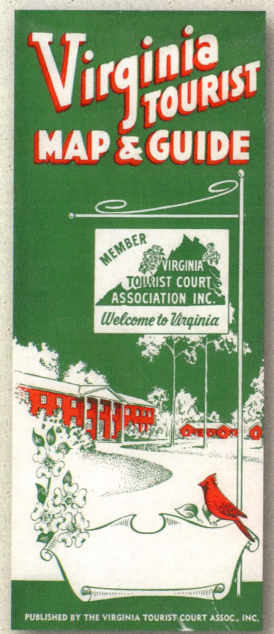

On June 16, 1941, local tourist court and tourist home owners announced the creation of the Virginia Tourism Association. The objectives of the Association were to improve the health and sanitation of tourist courts, to promote high standards among its members, to advertise member services, and to provide information for its members and the traveling public.[7] Though organized to improve quality and standards, associations were also interested in correcting the reputation tourist courts had gotten by assuring the public that motels affiliated with the associations were operating at a high standard. As such, motel associations helped the industry grow to the point where in 1962, in recognition of the importance of motels within the lodging industry, they merged with the American Hotel Association to become the American Hotel and Motel Association.[8]

Chapter 4

Tourist Homes – 1920-1950

In the 1920's and 30's, tourist homes were popular alternatives to tourist courts, especially in the east. In 1935, the *Hotel Monthly* reported that there were about 1,000 tourist homes registered in Richmond alone.[1] Tourist homes were operated by home owners whose properties were located along major highways both in rural and urban areas and were a source of income for homeowners during the Depression. Tourist homes differed from boarding houses in that they did not encourage extended stays, offering only overnight accommodations.

Cottage court owners considered tourist homes unfair competition; they rented comfortable rooms in nice houses with amenities and provided home cooking, all at much lower rates than either hotels or tourist courts could offer. It was largely the impact of tourist homes' competition with hotels and tourist courts that led to the first attempts in the 1930's for an industry-wide organization to establish standards and control prices.[2]

Gasoline rationing imposed during World War II greatly reduced tourist travel causing some tourist courts and other roadside businesses to fail. The August 11, 1942 *Richmond News Leader* reported that the results of a survey of tourist homes along Chamberlayne Avenue revealed that the reduction in tourists had been offset by an increase in weekend soldier visitors and lodgers in town on war business.[3] The article also noted that tourist homes on the edge of town were in danger of going out of business and, in fact, tourist homes largely died out following the war. Those that did survive added cottages and became tourist courts.

Tourist homes were a major business in this area, particularly during the 1930's, and especially along Chamberlayne Avenue, a stretch of Highway 1 that had it's own "Chamberlayne Avenue Tourist Club."[4] The following are examples of tourist homes that promoted their businesses with postcards along Highway 1 from the 1920's through the 1940's. Some have been demolished; some are still private homes.

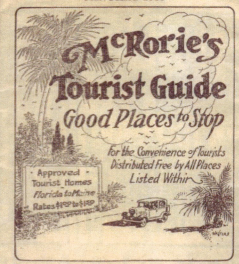

1935 McRorie's Tourist Guide

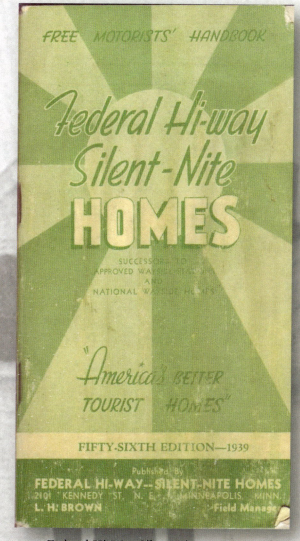

1939 Federal Hi-Way Silent Nite Homes Guide

Tourist Homes, After Early Knockout, Come Up Fighting

Week-End Soldiers Help to Fill Up Gaps

By ROBERT DIXON

Add to the list of those who make sacrifices to the war effort the names of that little band out on Chamberlayne Avenue whose tourist home business suffered a first-round knockdown when automobiles, tires and gasoline were rationed, only to come up fighting for new types of patrons.

A survey among the homes along Chamberlayne Avenue, from Lombardy Street to Norwood Avenue, today revealed that an actual tourist along that Parkway now is as scarce as an Aryan Jap. The consensus, however, of the proprietors (mostly women) was that their establishments will survive because of two unexpected windfalls. These are the groups of week-ending visiting soldiers and permanent roomers.

But, as for the tourists, they are gone until free markets in private transportation return. Business has been slashed about 60 per cent, with soldiers and roomers the only probable near-future patrons.

The tourist home may survive in Richmond proper, but surveys reveal that those beyond the local transportation systems have already begun to suffer the fates of the roadside cabins, pottery and antique shoppes and the roadside hotels with the homey airs, to say nothing of the big-time restaurants, one of which passed out on the northern fringe of Richmond soon after rationing began.

SCARCITY OF HELP

From reports made to Mrs. Oliver A. Chalifoux, president of the Chamberlayne Avenue Tourist Club, which is composed of most of the 40-odd tourist home proprietors in that area, it was learned every sleeping room and a few parlors and sleeping porches were occupied over last week-end. But week-end business will not continue to pay prosperity dividends, the proprietors say. Other difficulties increase their costs, among them the scarcity of help which now brings a wage premium.

The tourist home business on Chamberlayne Avenue was born of early depression days, when many of the well-to-do took in paying guests to augment diminished income. Later it grew to businesslike proportions when heavy traffic drove many large homeowners away and made their large establishments available for moderate rentals.

The business in recent years created many economic problems and was the object of several attacks by private homeowners. Settling these problems resulted in licensing the homes much as a hotel is licensed, according to the number of rooms, with those serving meals being forced to pay licenses similar to restaurants.

Rationing brought vital changes. Instead of 500 overnight guests in a single Summer month, one tourist home reported it had en-

Some Now Turning to Permanent Roomers

tertained less than 200. This home is operated by a woman who is not entirely dependent upon the overnight business. Another woman, who retained her home after the depression wiped her out financially, educated her two boys by operating a tourist business. The boys went to college. Two blue stars now show on the red, white and blue flag in a front window. One of the boys is in Australia.

SEES SACRIFICES

"Of course I'll try to keep our home," she said today. "It will mean making sacrifices in personal living, but it is our home, and we hope to make the grade."

Another woman, whose husband is in the service, is educating a daughter at a western conserva-

Concluded on Page 20

Richmond News Leader, August 11, 1942

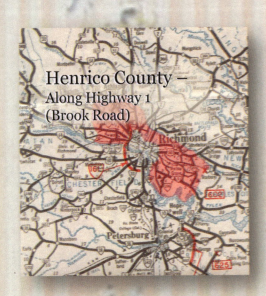

Henrico County –
Along Highway 1
(Brook Road)

Oakleigh Tourist Home

"A Modern Motel Tourist Home" and, according to the 1940 edition of the *American Motel Association Guide*, a "Large suburban home with all city conveniences plus the quiet of the country." [5] The owners of the Oakleigh advertised innerspring mattresses, steam heat, meals, and the fact that they were located back from the highway. The Oakleigh unlikely survived as a tourist home beyond 1945. It is no longer standing.

Richmond City –
North to South Along Highway 1
(Chamberlayne Avenue, Jefferson Davis Highway)

The Virginian
"A Guest Home of Charm". The Virginian offered private baths – if desired. Located at 4832 Chamberlayne Avenue, the home is still standing.

The Oasis
The Oasis, a "Modern Tourist Home", is still intact at 4810 Chamberlayne Avenue.

BROOK HILL COTTAGE, RICHMOND, VIRGINIA

Brook Hill Cottage

The Brook Hill Cottage, located at 4804 Chamberlayne Avenue, solicited overnight guests only and offered garage parking. Remodeled over the years, this tourist home is still standing. (Mike Uzel postcard)

The Richmond

Postmarked 1937, this postcard was sent by travelers heading south after passing through Baltimore and Washington, D.C. The Richmond offered 5 modern rooms with Beautyrest mattresses. Located at 4334 Chamberlayne Avenue, this home remains intact. (Mike Uzel postcard)

The Gables

The travelers who sent this postcard were in town to attend the Richmond Music Festival. "The picture of this house is where some of us spent the night. It was so nice". The Gables, located at 3914 Chamberlayne Avenue, has been demolished.

Redmont

The Redmont offered private and connecting baths, "automatic heat" and hot water. Located at 3814 Chamberlayne Avenue, the Redmont is no longer standing. (Mike Uzel postcard)

The Penfield Guest Home

The Penfield Guest Home advertised itself as a "strictly modern home" that was a quiet place that did not allow radios or pets. It did provide running water in each room, private baths, showers, garages, and parking space. The Penfield was located at 3810 Chamberlayne Avenue, now the site of an apartment building.

Park Lodge

The owners of the Park Lodge offered rooms with private baths, tubs and showers, oil heat, and meals that could be arranged; $3.30 for dinner and $1.25 for breakfast. (Travelers were expected to be gone by lunch time). The Park Lodge remains intact at 3806 Chamberlayne Avenue.

Tolvis Guest Home

The Tolvis Guest Home advertised itself as a "Home Away From Home", recommended by the American Automobile Association. Located at 3609 Chamberlayne Avenue, the Tolvis has been demolished. (Mike Uzel postcard)

Chamberlayne Lodge Tourist Home

The Chamberlayne Lodge Tourist Home was located "About 5 Squares South of Northern City Limits" at 3607 Chamberlayne Avenue. This house is no longer standing.

Kenton Arms

The Kenton Arms promoted its location within a quiet residential area of Richmond offering "the discriminating guest a private home operated under the personal supervision of the owner, Mrs. George Kenton Harper". Private and connecting baths, both showers and tubs, were available. This home is still standing at 3511 Chamberlayne Avenue. (Mike Uzel postcard)

House of Bruce

The House of Bruce offered "Modern and Distinctive Guest Accommodations" along with excellent meals, private and connecting baths, steam heat, and a garage. Located at 3500 Chamberlayne Avenue, this tourist home has been demolished.

Green Shutters Guest House

The Green Shutters Guest House, located at 3409 Chamberlayne Avenue, provided steam heat, running water in every room, baths, locked garages, and parking space. The Green Shutters has been demolished.

Park View Manor

The Park View Manor advertised moderate rates, free garage, and club breakfasts. Located at 3201 Chamberlayne Avenue, this tourist home has been demolished. (Mike Uzel postcard)

Magnolia Tourist Home

The Magnolia Tourist Home promoted clean and comfortable accommodations for travelers and tourists, private and semi-private baths, hot water at all times, and that it was only five minutes from historical points, theaters, and shopping areas in the city. Located at 3010 Chamberlayne Avenue, the home is still standing.

Tourist Rest

The Tourist Rest advertised itself as a member of the Virginia Travel Council and had its own advertising logo. The tourist home promoted its bright, well-ventilated rooms with outside exposures, innerspring mattresses, hot and cold baths, tubs and showers, garage and street parking. This home is still intact at 2912 Chamberlayne Avenue.

Clarke Guest House

The Clarke Guest House provide private baths, meals, and free garages. It was located at 2701 Chamberlayne Avenue but is no longer standing. (Mike Uzel postcard)

Kumfy Rest

Located in the vicinity of the 2100 block of Jefferson Davis Highway, the Kumfy Rest advertised what its name implied, "offering the best for the Overnight Guest. Beautyrest mattresses, Radios, Locked Garages, etc." The postcard contains a message dated 1938, "Spent the night here, very pleasant home." This house is no longer standing.

Chesterfield County –
Along Highway 1
(Jefferson Davis Highway)

Hill Top View

Hill Top View stood in the 17000 block of Jefferson Davis Highway. Along with modern conveniences, it offered free locked garages. This postcard contained the following message: "This was one of the places we stayed while we were gone. It was a good one." The Hill Top was located at what was later the site of a Tastee-Freeze owned by the Picardats, now the Tobacco and More Cigarette Outlet.

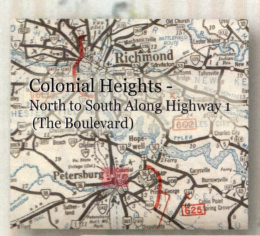

Colonial Heights -
North to South Along Highway 1 (The Boulevard)

Colonial Inn

This postcard, postmarked 1928, has no other advertising except for a picture of a man trimming hedges with a little girl watching, standing under the sign, "Colonial Inn, Rooms and Meals." The travelers who sent this postcard said, "Arrived here this evening and have just had a very delicious supper – Virginia style – oh boy…..We like this Colonial Inn but haven't time to stay longer." The Colonial Inn was located behind what is currently Pino's Italian Restaurant at 3416 Boulevard.

Boulevard Home

Boulevard Home stood at the intersection of F Avenue and the Boulevard but is no longer standing. It offered Beautyrest mattresses and modern conveniences.

Old Oaks

Located at 1217 Boulevard, the Old Oaks, now demolished, billed itself as, "The House Back from the Road." It offered private baths, hot water heat, locked garages, and the choicest of home cooked foods. On this postcard postmarked 1937, the traveler wrote, "This is one of our favorite stopping places."

New Brick Tourist Home

Located between Charlotte and Piedmont Avenues at 1214 Boulevard, the New Brick Tourist home advertised running water in each room, steam heat, baths and showers with hot water at "all times ", and home cooked meals. Travelers were alerted to watch for the neon arrow. This tourist home, owned by Mrs. J.A. Picardat, was later renamed the Roses of Picardy and continued to expand through the 1960's becoming a multi-building motel. The New Brick Tourist Home remains intact. (Mike Uzel postcard)

2012 View

Maple Manor

Located on the Boulevard next door to the New Brick Tourist Home, Maple Manor advertised "Real Virginia Ham and Chicken Dinners" along with Beautyrest mattresses, steam heat, running water in rooms, and free locked garages. In operation beginning in the 1930's, Maple Manor later became part of the Roses of Picardy Motel complex and is still intact.

2012 View

Westover Guest House

The Westover Guest House boasted its modern conveniences, breakfasts, and locked garages. Located at the intersection of the Boulevard and Westover Street, this tourist home is still standing and is currently the offices of the Lundie Insurance Center. (Mike Uzel postcard)

Peggy's Tourist Inn

Located at 618 Boulevard, Peggy's Tourist Inn featured free garages and modern conveniences. This tourist home is no longer standing, its site now occupied by a Cook Out fast food restaurant.

Westover Guest House
2012 View

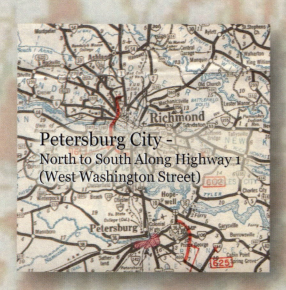

Petersburg City -
North to South Along Highway 1
(West Washington Street)

Folly Castle Inn

The Folly Castle Inn, an historic structure dating from 1763, became a tourist home in the 1930's offering accommodations including meals and parking. This structure is still standing at 323 West Washington Street.

Indiana Inn/Blue Heaven Guest Home

The Indiana Inn, at 1446 West Washington Street, was a 1930's tourist home that was later renamed the Blue Heaven Guest Home. It featured innerspring beds, steam heat, garages, and parking. This home is no longer standing.

Shady Rest Motel

Located at 1454 West Washington Street, the Shady Rest offered convenience to the "South's historical center", steam heat, innerspring mattresses, and lighted parking. Large groups were welcome. This home is no longer standing.

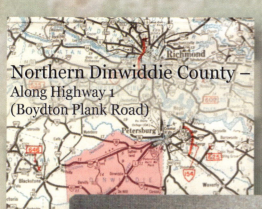

Northern Dinwiddie County –
Along Highway 1
(Boydton Plank Road)

Shadow Lawn

Shadow Lawn operated as a tourist home in the 1930's south of Petersburg along Highway 1. It featured modern accommodations and meals. Shadow Lawn is no longer standing.

Chapter 5

Motor Courts, Auto Courts, Tourist Courts, and Motels – 1940 to 1970

By 1950 the cottage court style had become dated, being replaced by "motor courts", a different design featuring integrated units adjoining each other, the style that would come to be universally be called "motel." Motor courts were single storied, were normally configured in U or L shapes, had separate buildings for guest reception, dining rooms, or gift shops, and were designed so that guests could park right at their room door.

The use of the word "motel" came to be more widely used after World War II though some owners continued to call their establishments motor courts, tourists courts, auto courts, or other popular terms.

The following are examples of the first motor courts and motels built in the area in the 1950's, the "golden age" of motels. Owned and operated locally, they would, in time, compete with chain motels or become owned by large corporations. Many are still in existence and continue to function as motels.

1958 Superior Courts Guide

1951-52 American Motel Association Guide

1950-51 Quality Courts United Guide

Henrico County –
North to South Along Highway 1
(Brook Road)

Princess Lee Motel

The Princess Lee Motel, built in 1952, is located at 9004 Brook Road and contained many of the amenities that were new for its time including a television in each room and a swimming pool. It featured 62 rooms, "40 in French Provincial Décor." The Princess Lee Motel is now a Knight's Inn, a lodging chain first incorporated in 1973.

2012 View

Cavalier Manor Motel

The Cavalier Manor Motel was built in 1953 and advertised its tile baths, wall-to-wall carpeting, and telephones in each room. A swimming pool was added later. In the late 1960's, it became a member of the Best Western Motels, one of the more successful motel referral chains that later became a franchise. By 1960, motels along Brook Road began providing directions from I-95 (Parham Road Exit) to draw travelers. The Cavalier Motel is still in business at 8827 Brook Road.

Brook Run Lodge

Built in the 1940's, Brook Run Lodge offered 52 rooms with tiled baths, air conditioning, landscaped grounds, and was "only 15 minutes from downtown Richmond." The Brook Run Lodge was located at 5221 Brook Road, later becoming the site of the Holiday Inn of Richmond.

Richmond City –
North to South Along Highway 1 (Azalea Avenue, Chamberlayne Avenue, Belvidere Street, & Jefferson Davis Highway)

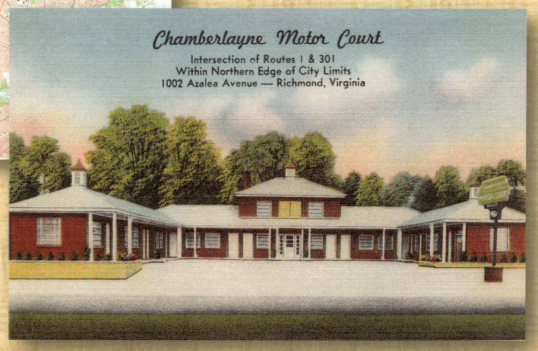

Chamberlayne Motor Court

Built in 1953, the Chamberlayne Motor Court was designed in what was to become a standard U-shaped, one story building. This motor court was one of the earlier lodging establishments inside the Richmond City limits designed to cater to motorists. Located at 1002 Azalea Avenue, the Chamberlayne Motel remains in business.

2012 View

Richmond Motel

The Richmond Motel was built in 1953, "In the Heart of Town." It offered travelers 70 modern rooms, tiled baths, restaurants nearby, and easy access to business and shopping districts. Television and air conditioning were optional however. The Richmond Motel is still in business at 2600 Chamberlayne Avenue.

Town Motel

The Town Motel, built in the early 1960's, featured two stories, a precursor to multi-storied motels that became more common after 1960 called "motor inns." Located at 601 South Belvidere Street, the motel featured rooms with air conditioning, TV, and convenience to downtown. The motel was demolished in the 1980's. The property is now the site of the Virginia Housing Development Authority, next to the Virginia War Memorial.

City Motel

The City Motel was built in 1958 in a typical U shaped, one-story design. In the 1960's, the motel expanded and a two-story addition was added along with a separate restaurant. The motel featured air conditioning "year round", showers and tiled baths, and proximity to the city. The motel is still functioning and is located at 3015-23 Jefferson Davis Highway.

Jefferson Davis Motel
Opened in 1952, the Jefferson Davis Motel offered "Ultra modern units" and "The South's finest city fire and police protection." It also advertised air foam mattresses, a recent alternative to innerspring mattresses, and a restaurant. This motel is still doing business at 3314 Jefferson Davis Highway.

Jefferson Davis Motel
2012 View

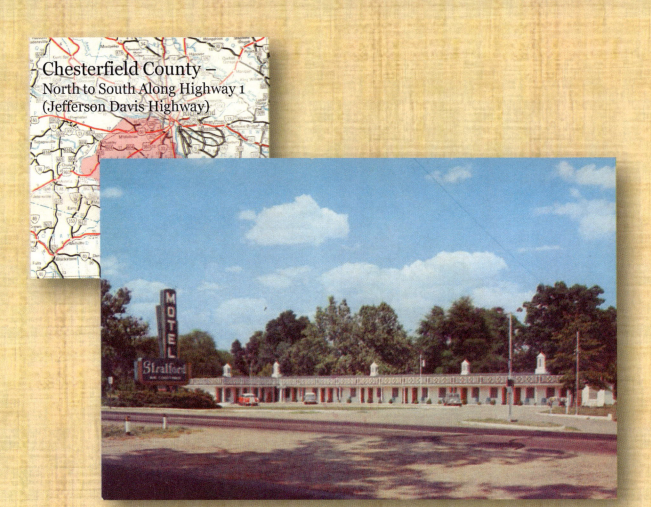

Stratford Motel

The Stratford Motel was built in 1957 across from what was then the Richmond Quartermaster Depot, now the Defense Logistics Agency-Aviation. It featured "15 modernly furnished rooms-Complete with television-... Beautyrest box springs & mattresses-Wall to wall carpet-Private Ceramic tile baths-City water-Cross ventilation-Hot water heating." In 1958, the Richmond-Petersburg Turnpike began operation, so motels along Jefferson Davis Highway began providing directions from the Turnpike. Travelers were advised to take either Exit 7 (Falling Creek exit, now Chippenham Highway) or the Willis Road Exit 6A (today's Exit 64). The Stratford is still in business at 8115 Jefferson Davis Highway.

2012 View

Martha-Kay Motel

The Martha-Kay Motel offered tiled baths, tubs and showers, wall-to-wall carpet, air conditioning, and television. There was also a restaurant nearby. Built in 1953, the motel later advised travelers driving the Richmond-Petersburg Turnpike to take Exit 6A, (today's Willis Road Exit 64) turn right and go 2 blocks. Located at 8811 Jefferson Davis Highway, the Martha-Kay is still in business.

2012 View

Virginian Motel

The Virginian Motel, an 18 unit motel built in 1951, offered travelers air foam mattresses and pillows, wall-to-wall carpet, county water, air conditioning, and fireproof construction. Improvements were made in 1961 to include the addition of a heated swimming pool, later removed. The Virginian Motel is still in business at 8924 Jefferson Davis Highway.

2012 View

Snow White Motel

Built in 1955, the Snow White Motel advertised "Modern, Beautifully furnished units Air Conditioned" – Television and Swimming Pool", since removed. The Snow White Motel remains in business located at 9301 Jefferson Davis Highway.

2012 View

White House Motor Lodge

The White House Motor Lodge was built in 1952, and with 54 units was the largest motel built in Chesterfield County in the 1950's. [1] The motel offered air conditioning, television, an adjoining restaurant, and at one time provided guests a swimming pool. After the Richmond-Petersburg Turnpike was built, the motel provided directions from Exits 6 and 6A, today's Exits 61 (Route 10) and 64 (Willis Road). The White House is still doing business at 9401 Jefferson Davis Highway.

Homestead Motel

The Homestead Motel was built in 1952 in a standard L-shaped one story design. A swimming pool was added later. The Homestead stood on the site now occupied by John Tyler Community College at 13151 Jefferson Davis Highway.

Patrick Henry Motel

"This is where we stayed the second night and was a very nice place and was very quiet for a motel" so wrote a traveler in the 1950's on a postcard from the Patrick Henry Motel. The Patrick Henry featured "20 spacious rooms" with air foam mattresses, heat, and tubs and showers. Built in the early 1950's in an L-shaped, one story design, the Patrick Henry later added an additional wing, a restaurant, and swimming pool. Located at 13201 Jefferson Davis Highway, and at one time operated by the Vogenburgers, the establishment is still in business as a Budget Inn Motel.

2012 View

Par 3 Motel

In 1956, the Oak View Motel was completely renovated from the cottage court style to a more modern motel design. In 1963, it was renamed the Par 3 Motel, operated by the Par 3 Country Club Motels Inc., and included an adjacent golf course. The golf course is gone but the Par 3 is still in business as apartments at 16800 Jefferson Davis Highway.

1979 View
(Virginia Department of Historic Resources)

2012 View

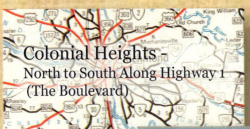

Swift Creek Motel

The Swift Creek Motel was built in 1953 in two sections across the street from one another (east and west) that together contained 31 units. It also featured the Swift Creek Farms Restaurant located on the western property. The motel offered television, baths, and showers and advertised the fact that its restaurant was recommended by Duncan Hines. The motel is still standing and operating as apartments at 3618 Boulevard. Little remains of the western units but the restaurant is still in business at 3620 Boulevard, currently as Carrini Italian Pizza and Restaurant.

2012 View, East Section

AAA SWIFT CREEK FARMS FAMOUS RESTAURANT — MOTOR COURT

2012 View, West Section

Roses of Picardy

Beginning as tourist homes in the 1930's called Maple Manor and the New Brick Tourist Home, the Roses of Picardy grew to become a motel of mixed designs that included hotel, cottage, and motel style accommodations. The 1950 *Virginia Tourist Guide* described the Roses of Picardy as a tourist home and cottages with steam heat, private baths, tubs and showers and a restaurant and theater across the street. The Roses of Picardy is still standing at 1214 Boulevard and now accommodates a variety of shops and businesses.

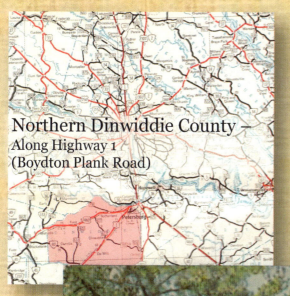

Northern Dinwiddie County –
Along Highway 1
(Boydton Plank Road)

The Georgian Motel

The Georgian Motel was built in early 1950's in a style that proved popular in this area; a colonial style architecturally designed centerpiece with rooms extending outward. The Georgian is located seven miles south of Petersburg at 9222 Boydton Plank Road and offered modern facilities and fine dining. The Georgian was demolished in 2104.

Georgian Motel
2012 View

Chapter 6

The Green Book

For African Americans traveling in the first half of the 20th Century, finding a place to stay was often a problem. In 1936, Victor H. Green, a postal employee and civic leader from Harlem, began publishing a travel guide for blacks traveling in the New York City area and later expanded it to cover the entire United States, Canada, and Mexico.[1] The *Negro Motorist Green Book*, simply called the "*Green Book*", listed hotels, motels, tourist homes, restaurants, and other services where blacks would be welcome. The guide was updated yearly and depended on information from correspondents in the field to add to the list of businesses. It was not inclusive but served to supplement the word of mouth and social networks that provided travel information.

The 1949 edition of the *Green Book* listed several establishments along Highway 1 between Richmond and Petersburg where black travelers could find lodging. Except for the Colbrook Motel, all have been demolished.

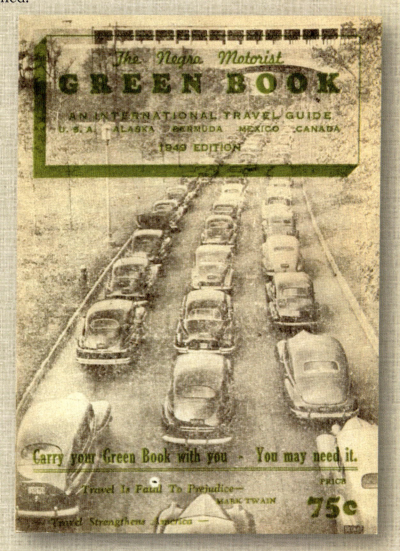

Petersburg Hotels:
  The Walker House, 116 South Street
  Colbrook Inn, U.S. Highway No. 1

Richmond Hotels:
  Harris, 200 East Clay Street
  Eggleston (Miller's), 2nd and Leigh Streets

Richmond Tourist Homes:
  Mrs. E. Brice, 14 West Clay Street
  Y.W.C.A., 515 North 7th Street
  Jack's, on Route 1, 6 miles north of Richmond

Colbrook Inn/Motel

Located at 13916 Jefferson Davis Highway, the Colbrook Inn was built in 1946 in the motor court style of construction and was one of the motels listed in the *Green Book* that welcomed black travelers. The motel is still in operation.

The Colbrook was established, owned, and operated by Mr. William E. Brooks, Sr., an original member of the Tuskegee Airmen, the all-black Army Air Force squadron of World War II fame. Mr. Brooks owned the Colbrook from 1946 until 1983.

2012 Views

(Chesterfield County Historical Society image)

Motel Chesterfield

The Motel Chesterfield was located near the intersection of Route 10 and Jefferson Davis Highway. Not listed in the *Green Book*, it was a two story motel and restaurant owned by the Friend family.[2] This motel is no longer standing.

In the introduction to the *Green Book*, Victor Green wrote "There will be a day sometime in the near future when this guide will not have to be published. That is when we as a race will have equal opportunities and privileges in the United States."[3] With the passage of the Civil Rights Act in 1964, the *Green Book* ceased publication.

Chapter 7

Interstates and Motel Chains – 1950 to 1975

In 1955 the Richmond-Petersburg Turnpike Authority was established to build a 35 mile four-lane toll road from northern Dinwiddie County to Highway 301 in Henrico County. Completed in 1958, the Turnpike soon became integrated with the interstate highway system, becoming a portion of I-95 and I-85. [1]

Motel owners along Highway 1 had been concerned upon hearing the plans for the Turnpike, fearing that travelers would be less inclined to leave the new highway to find lodging. Their concerns were realized as the impact on the motels was immediate and, for some, terminal. Not only were owners competing with each other for business, they also soon began to compete with hotel-motel chains. This business model gained popularity in the 1950's, made most successful by Holiday Inns but also included such franchises as Howard Johnson's, Ramada Inn, and Best Western which all appeared in the 1960's. These franchise chains, along with other local private corporations established to build travel lodging, focused their efforts on building motels at, or close to, the Turnpike exits.

This marked the beginning of the end of the independent, single family-owned motels along Highway 1. By the 1970's, those that survived tended to depend on transient business or rented their units as budget apartments for extended stays and came to be owned as part of local corporations. Few motels were built along Highway 1 after 1958.

The following are some of the earlier motels built along the Richmond-Petersburg Turnpike. Some are still standing and over the years have gone through different names and management; some have been demolished. The original exit numbers of the Turnpike are used to indicate their locations, along with the current exit numbers (in parentheses), and are listed north to south.

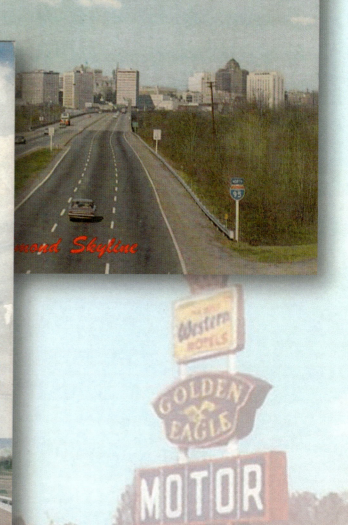

Turnpike Exits 17 & 16
(I-95 Exits 82 & 81 – Chamberlayne Avenue/Brook Road)

Schrafft's Virginia Inn

Located at Exit 17 at 5701 Chamberlayne Avenue just before Highway 301 joins Highway 1, Schrafft's Virginia Inn was built in 1963, accessible from the Turnpike. This motel is still standing and doing business as a Days Inn Motel.

Holiday Inn of Richmond

The Holiday Inn motel chain, founded by Kemmon Wilson in 1952, marked a radical change in the travel lodging industry. [2] Offering consistent quality, family-friendly prices, and clever marketing, Holiday Inns became the most successful and most recognizable motels in the 1950's and '60's. The Holiday Inn of Richmond was built in the late 1950's at 5221 Brook Road near the I-95 Exits 81 and 82. The motel was remodeled and renamed numerous times over the years but in 2015 was demolished.

2012 View

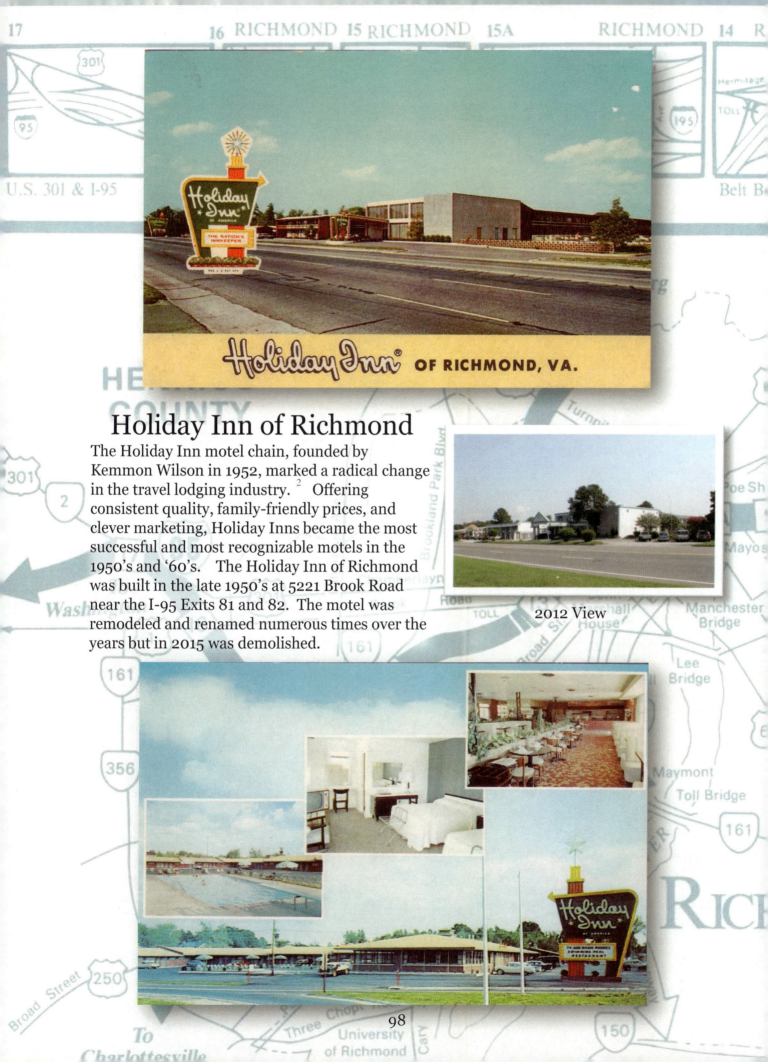

Turnpike Exit 14
(I-95 Exit 78 – Boulevard)

Holiday Inn – Richmond #2
Another Holiday Inn, located at 1501 Robin Hood Road, was built in 1961 situated at the Boulevard Exit. Most of this motel has been demolished.

Quality Motel Intown
Quality Courts and Inns began as a referral organization in 1941 but by 1950, had become a chain.[3] The Quality Motel Intown was built in 1963 at 1600 Robin Hood Road at the Boulevard Exit. This motel is still standing and operating as a Scottish Inn, a motel chain established in 1973 and now part of the Red Carpet Inn franchise.[4]

Turnpike Exits 13 & 12
(I-95 Exits 76 A & B – Belvidere & Chamberlayne)

Mark Monroe Motor Hotel/ Sheraton Motor Inn

By the 1950's, hotel corporations came to accept that the automobile had forever changed how America traveled and that the motoring public had certain expectations about lodging. Hotels began to offer parking and other amenities to lure travelers into cities and to acknowledge what had become the norm; more people were traveling by car than by train. A new style of city hotel emerged; the motor inn, a motel that offered a hotel appearance and amenities.

Located on the southeast corner of Belvidere and Franklin Streets, the route of Highway 1 through Richmond, the Mark Monroe Motor Hotel (above) was built in 1959 in the motor inn style. It was later purchased by the Sheraton Hotel chain which, in the 1950's and '60's, was purchasing properties to expand their role in motor lodging. Renamed the Sheraton Motor Inn (below), the property was later demolished and replaced by an apartment building.

Turnpike Exit 6A (I-95 Exit 64 – Willis Road)

Ramada Inn

The Ramada Inn brand was established in 1954 as a southwestern motel chain but by 1960 could be found throughout the United States.[5] The Ramada Inn at 2126 Willis Road at Exit 6A (Exit 64), was built in 1973. It has gone through several renovations and name changes but continues to operate as a motel, currently an American Best Value Inn.

Econo Travel Motor Hotel

Later renamed Econo-Lodge, the Econo Travel Motor Hotel budget chain was a Norfolk-based corporation established in 1972.[6] Located at 2125 Willis Road, this motel was one of the first built by the chain in 1972 and is still in operation. (All Econo Travel Motor Hotel postcards had the same image reflecting the chain's standardization; only the location information on the back of the card was different).

Mark Warren Motel

Built in 1960, the Mark Warren Motel has changed ownership and renamed several times during its history. In the mid-1960's, the motel became a member of the Quality Court chain, called Quality Inn South and was later part of the Best Western referral chain and renamed the Golden Eagle Motor Inn. The motel was also once called the Golden Empire Motor Inn. Located at 2301 Willis Road, the motel is currently a VIP Inn.

Economy House Motel

Built in 1963, the Economy House Motel remained in business as late as 2010. Only a portion of the restaurant and office remain at 3302 Willis Road.

Turnpike Exit 6
(I-95 Exit 61 – Route 10)

Howard Johnson Motor Lodge

By 1954, Howard Johnsons, a 1920's roadside restaurant chain, had expanded to include motels.[7] The Chester Howard Johnson Motor Lodge was built in the late 1950's and was located in the 2400 block of West Hundred Road at the northwest intersection of Route 10 and I-95. In 1985, Marriot purchased the Howard Johnson Company and sold off the motel side of the business.[8] The Chester Howard Johnson Motor Lodge was demolished in the late 1980's but the property is currently occupied by a Fairfield Inn, a chain established in 1986, and a Country Inn and Suites, part of the Carlson Hotel Group.[9]

Holiday Inn, Chester

Built in 1969, the Chester Holiday Inn has undergone several renovations and name changes over the years. Located at 2401 West Hundred Road (Route 10) it is currently operating as a Suburban Extended Stay Hotel, part of the Choice Hotels chain.

Turnpike Exit 5
(I-95 Exit 58 – Walthall)

Indian Hills Motel

Built through the efforts of a limited partnership in 1973, the Indian Hills Motel was located at the northwest section of the Walthall Exit. The motel has been demolished except for one wing which was incorporated into the current Interstate Inn now occupying the site.

Old Stage Motor Lodge

Built in the 1960's by a locally owned corporation, the Old Stage Motor Lodge was located at the southeast corner of the Walthall Exit Interchange. The motel was demolished when the exit was redeveloped in the early 2000's and is currently the site of a variety of automobile dealerships.

Turnpike Exit 3
(I-95 Exit 52 – Bank & Washington Streets, Petersburg)

Howard Johnson's Motor Lodge

Built in 1969, the Petersburg Howard Johnson's is located east of the Turnpike between Washington and Wythe's Streets and is currently operating as a Travelodge Motel.

Holiday Inn Downtown

The Holiday Inn Downtown was built in 1971, located east of I-95 at 501 East Washington Street. The motel was demolished in 2014.

America House Motor Inn

The America House Motor Inn is located at 405 East Washington Street. Built in the 1960's, the America House was one of two built in Virginia; the other is located on the Eastern Shore. The motel is currently unoccupied.

Turnpike Exit 2 (I-95 Exit 50 – Routes 301 & 460)

Heart of Petersburg Motel/ Camara Inn

Built in the 1960's, the Heart of Petersburg Motel was located at 815 South Crater Road bordering the Petersburg National Battlefield. It was later remodeled and renamed the Camara Inn (below). The motel is still standing and doing business as a Flagship Inn.

Golden Empire Motor Inn ca. 1970, originally the Mark Warren Motel
Willis Road, I-95 Exit 64

Chapter 8

U.S. Highway 301 – Petersburg Motels

U.S. Highway 301 appeared in Virginia in 1932 running from Petersburg south through Emporia to North Carolina. By 1941, the highway had been extended north to Delaware, sharing the roadway with U.S. Highway 1 between Petersburg and Richmond. With the opening of the highway travelers going southbound were given a choice at Petersburg where Highways 1 and 301 split. Judging from the number of postcards published by Petersburg motels, most travelers chose Highway 301. When the Interstate Highway System was built, I-95 continued south from Petersburg paralleling Highway 301, while I-85 paralleled Highway 1. [1]

The following motels were located along Highway 301 in Petersburg and northern Prince George County from 1930 to 1970. The completion of I-95, coupled with the urbanization along South Crater Road beginning in the 1970's, led to the end of most of these motels.

Petersburg/Northern Prince George County –
North to South Along Highway 301
(South Crater Road)

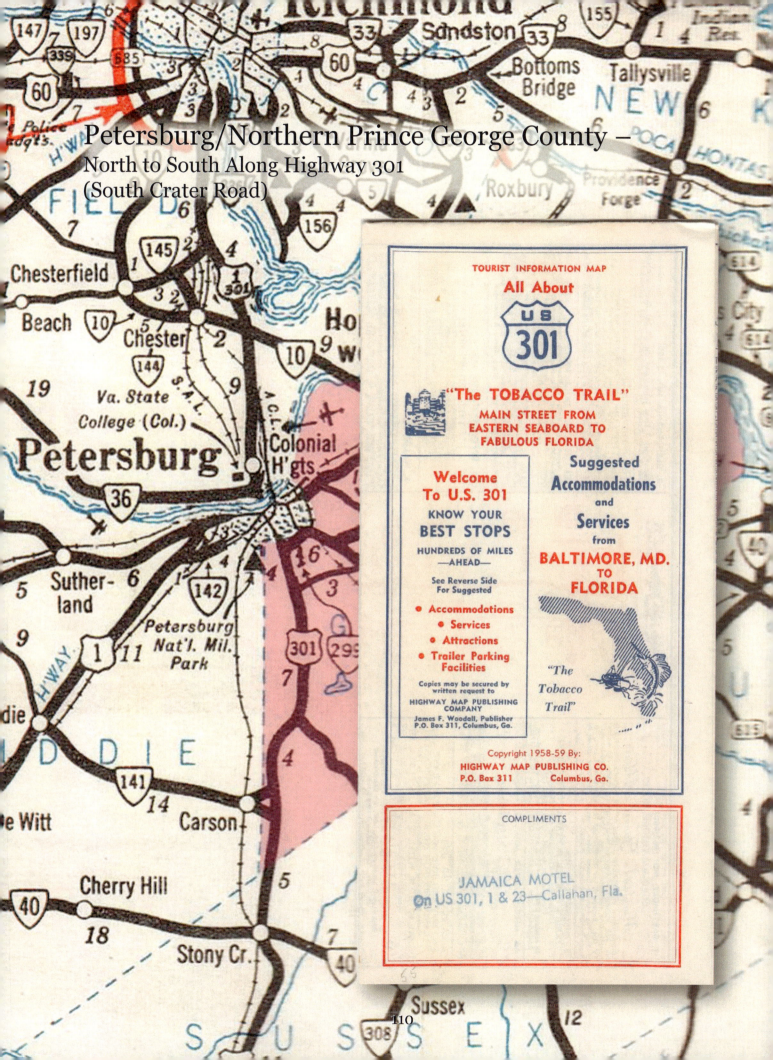

Cottage Courts – 1920 to 1950

Windsor Court

Built in the 1940's the Windsor Court contained 10 "Modern Units with Private Baths", along with showers and radiant heating. The Windsor Court was located in the vicinity of the 3300 block of South Crater Road, now the site of various commercial enterprises.

Bancroft Motel

The Bancroft Motel had a typical cottage court design and offered separate cottages with modern rooms, showers, and a location back from the highway. Built in the 1940's but no longer standing, this tourist court was located in the 10500 block of South Crater Road.

Brook's Tourist Court/ Motel Arthur

The Brook's Tourist Court was located in northern Prince George County along Highway 301 south of today's I-95 Exit 45. It featured brick, insulated, and steam-heated cottages. The tourist court was later renamed the Motel Arthur. Portions of this tourist court are still visible at 14205-14213 South Crater Road.

2012 View

Tourist Homes – 1920-1950

Sycamore Tourist Home

The Sycamore Tourist Home, located at 606 South Sycamore Street (U.S. Highway 301), advertised itself as six blocks south of Highway 1. The house is still a private residence.

Strother House

The Strother House, located eight blocks south of Highway 1 on South Sycamore Street offered modern accommodations, dining room, and free locked garages. This tourist home is no longer standing.

Heath's Court

This "I" shaped court, named for the owners, featured eight units with Simmons Beautyrest mattresses, tiled bath and showers, and television. Built in the early 1950's, Heath's Motel was located in the vicinity of the 10500 block of South Crater Road but is no longer standing.

Continental Motel

The Continental Motel was built in the late 1950's and offered radiant heat, air conditioning, and free television. The travelers who sent this postcard in 1965 spent their first night at the Continental while driving south to Florida. Located at 11800 South Crater Road, the Continental Motel is still in business.

Ellwyn Motel

"Hi Folks: Made 503 miles today. Sure are tired." So wrote a traveler who stayed at the Ellwyn Motel in 1955. The Ellwyn featured 20 modern units with wall-to-wall carpeting, tiled baths, air conditioning, swimming pool, restaurant, and a guest lounge with a fireplace. No longer standing, the Ellwyn was located near the South Crater Road/I-95 Exit 45.

Hollycrest Motel

Built in 1952, the Hollycrest Motel was designed in the L shape style. Located at 14804 South Crater Road, the Hollycrest remains intact but is in ruins.

The Claremont

The Claremont, on U.S. Highway 301, was an expansive 51 unit motel built in the early 1950's located 10 miles south of Petersburg. One traveler wrote home in 1957 remarking, "This is a deluxe place." The Claremont advertised its swimming pool, restaurant, and offered television and telephones in every room. This motel is still intact at 17400 South Crater Road but is unoccupied.

2012 View

Interstates and Motel Chains – 1950 to 1975

Quality Court Motel, South

Built in the 1960's, the Quality Court South at Exit 45, I-95, Route 301, featured 75 rooms including family rooms and bridal suites. Resort-type motel amenities such as a putting green, tennis court, shuffleboard, an Olympic-sized swimming pool, and lawn games, were also included. Remodeled over the years, the motel is now a part of the Howard Johnson Motel chain. The Steven Kent Restaurant is still in business.

Holiday Inn of Petersburg

One of the several Holiday Inns built in the area during the late 1950's, the Holiday Inn of Petersburg was located nine miles south of the city at Exit 41, I-95, Routes 35, 156, and 301. Though still standing at Exit 41 at 16600 Sunnybrook Road, the motel last operated as a Knights Inn but is currently unoccupied.

2012 View

Congress Inn/Bollingbrook Inn

Established in 1960, the Congress Inn franchise was short-lived, lasting until the 1980's. [2] The Congress Inn built at Exit 41 had 70 rooms, a restaurant, swimming pool, banquet and convention facilities, gas station, and pony rides available for guests. The motel later left the Congress Inn franchise and was renamed the Bollingbrook Inn. The motel is still in business as the Econo Lodge South.

Chapter 9

Epilog

Since the 1970's, the motel/hotel hospitality business has continued to prosper along the Richmond-Petersburg corridor. The motel/hotel building boom in the 1980's was an unprecedented occurrence noted by the *Richmond Times Leader*.[1] The later surge of lodging construction sparked by the expansion of Fort Lee in 2005 left Highway 1 largely unaffected; the focus of the construction was along the interstates and within urban areas. Since I-95 became operational in 1958, very few motels have been constructed along Highway 1. Those that were, however, remain in business.

The Sleep Inn and Country Inn and Suites
Willis Road Exit 64

Along Brook Road, three motels were built after 1958: The Town Motel at 5214 Brook Road (1961), the Alpine Motel at 7009 Brook Road (1990), and the Broadway Motel at 8302 Brook Road (1992).

There were two motels built in Richmond in 1994 along Chamberlayne Avenue: the Beacon Motel (now the Enys Motel), 2929 Chamberlayne Avenue, and the Belmont Motel, 2301 Chamberlayne Avenue.

Between 1989 and 1992, four motels were built along Jefferson Davis Highway within the Richmond City limits: the Southside Motel, 4310 Jefferson Davis Highway (1989), the Rainbow Motel, 4611 Jefferson Davis Highway (1990), Deluxe Inn, 4601 Jefferson Davis Highway (1991), and the Relax Inn, 3411 Jefferson Davis Highway (1992).

In 2006, the Executive Inn & Suites at 8107 Jefferson Davis Highway was built across from the Defense Logistic Agency-Aviation, the only motel built along Highway 1 in Chesterfield County since 1958.* The majority of motels still operating along Highway 1 continue to be those built between 1950 and 1958, surviving as budget extended-stay or apartment-style lodging alternatives that do not rely on the traveling public for business.

---

*In 2001, an Intown Suites was built at 2601 Perdue Spring Drive just off of Jefferson Davis Highway in Chester. Intown Suites is an extended-stay establishment that caters to guests requiring weekly or longer stays.

The commercial landscape along Highway 1 between Richmond and Petersburg has been modified constantly over the years as the new replaces the old. Even as this was being written, the last remnants of the Colony Inn, once one of the premier motels along Jefferson Davis Highway, were demolished to make room for a new chapter in the highway's history. The last 20 years have also seen the disappearance of other interesting and ornate motels such as Moore's Brick Cottages, Dutch Gap Tourist Court, and the Ye Blue Tartane. It is to be expected that the motels and tourist courts that remain will also, in time, be removed to make way for new development. Because of this, the information in this work is accurate only as of 2016. And as history has shown, the motels built in the last 20 years will also at some point be demolished or renovated to meet the demands of the times. But unlike the motels of the past, there will be no postcards to provide evidence of their existence.   By the 1970's, most motels stopped providing free postcards for their guests. The motel business had become dominated by franchises and corporations who didn't use postcards as a marketing tool and by the 1990's, the internet and instant communications made the idea of giving away postcards to customers so that they could write home seem ….quaint.

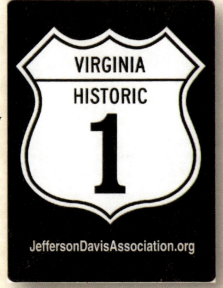

In 2010, U.S. Highway 1 was designated an Historic Highway by the Virginia General Assembly, a recognition of the importance of the highway not only to Virginia but to the entire nation. From a through-route used by Native Americans to motorists in the mid-20th century, the route of Highway 1 was the most important north-south route on the east coast. The historic designation was made possible largely through the efforts of the Jefferson Davis Association, an organization established in 1992.   Its mission is to promote the historic, cultural, and economic benefits of Highway 1, America's Main Street.   The Association developed initiatives to revitalize the Jefferson Davis corridor, focusing on beautification, commercial enterprise, and the historic sites along the highway. The intent is to lure tourists off of I-95 and to experience what Historic Highway 1 has to offer, as it has for tourists for the last 90 years, and to….

"Spend a Night on the Pike."

Endnotes

Chapter 1 - Prologue

[1] History of Roads in Virginia: "The Most Convenient Wayes". (Richmond: Commonwealth of Virginia, 2006) 17-23

[2] "Transportation Indicators for Motor Vehicles and Airlines: 1900-2001". <http://www.census.gov/statab/hist/HS-41.pdf>

[3] " 'Different' Road Camps". The Richmond News Leader. 21 Dec. 1939: 10

[4] "Police Check Tourist Camps in County". The Richmond News Leader. 11 Jul. 1940: 2

Chapter 2 - Camps, Cabins, Inns, and Cottage Courts – 1920 to 1950

[1] Jakle, John A., et al. The Motel in America. (Baltimore and London: The Johns Hopkins University Press, 1996) 39.

[2] Ridout, John. "A History of the Route 1 Corridor". (Chesterfield County Office of Revitalization, July 2006)

[3] Quality Courts United Guide, Revised 1945. (Quality Courts United Inc. 1945).

[4] Chesterfield Plus. 3 Oct. 1990.

[5] Hines, Duncan. Lodging for the Night. (Bowling Green: Adventures in Good Eating, Inc., 1946) 259.

[6] From notes, Virginia Department of Historic Resources, 12 Feb 2012.

[7] United Motor Courts Guide. 1937.

[8] Finest Tourist Homes, De-Luxe Cottage Courts, Excellent Restaurants. (East Orange, NJ: American Motel Association, 1940).

[9] Virginia Tourist Court Guide. (Virginia: Virginia Tourist Court Association, 1950).

[10] Virginia Tourist Court Guide.

[11] Virginia Tourist Court Guide.

[12] Virginia Tourist Court Guide.

[13] Hines. 262.

Chapter 3 - Camps of Crime – Camps of Quality

[1] "Camps of Crime". <u>American Magazine</u>. Feb 1940: 14
<http://en.wikipedia.org/wiki/Motel>

[2] "Finds Tourist Camps Often Put to Immoral Use". <u>The Richmond News Leader.</u> 21 Dec. 1939: 1-2

[3] "Conditions At Road Camps". <u>The Richmond News Leader</u>. 21 Dec. 1939: 10

[4] "Tourist Camp Definition Stumps Legislative Group". <u>The Richmond News Leader.</u> 2 Feb. 1940: 1

[5] "Tourist Camp Bill To Cut Teeth In June". <u>The Richmond News Leader</u>. 21 Mar. 1940: 5

[6] Jakle. 131-133

[7] "State Operators of Tourist Courts and Home Organize". <u>The Richmond News Leader</u>. 16 Jun. 1941: 15

[8] Jakle. 133

Chapter 4 - Tourist Homes – 1920-1950

[1] Jakle. 36

[2] Belasco, Warren James. <u>America on the Road: From Autocamp to Motel, 1910-1945.</u> (Baltimore and London: The Johns Hopkins University Press, 1979) 153.

[3] "Tourist Homes, After Early Knockout, Come Up Fighting". <u>The Richmond News Leader.</u> 11 Aug. 1942: 3

[4] "Tourist Homes".

[5] <u>Finest Tourist Homes.</u>

Chapter 5 - Motor Courts, Auto Courts, Tourist Courts, and Motels – 1940 to1970

[1] Ridout.

Chapter 6 - The Green Book

[1] McGee, Celia. "The Open Road Wasn't Quite Open to All". 12 August 2012. <http://www.nytimes.com/2010/08/23/books/23green.html?_r=1>

[2] "Interview with Otha Lee Taylor – Reminiscence – Life on the Pike." <u>Village News.</u> 28 Jul 28, 2010.

[3] <u>The Negro Motorist Green Book</u>. (New York: Victor H. Green, 1949) 1

Chapter 7 - Interstates and Motel Chains – 1950 to 1975

[1] Kozel, Scott M. "Richmond Interstates and Expressways". 30 July 2007. <http://www.roadstothefuture.com/Richmond_Interstate_Expy.html>

[2] Jakle. 262-265

[3] Jakle. 162-165

[4] Jakle, 197-198

[5] Jakle. 182-184

[6] Jakle. 170-171

[7] Jakle. 155-156

[8] Jakle. 184-187

[9] Jakle. 203-204

Chapter 8 - U.S. Highway 301 – Petersburg Motels

[1] "Virginia Highways Page US Routes 1 and Branches". 22 July 2007. <http://www.angelfire.com/va3/mapmikey/US1.html>

[2] Jakle. 173

Chapter 9 - Epilog

[1] "Hotel Boom Unprecedented, Observers Say". <u>The Richmond News Leader.</u> 20 Apr. 1984: pgs 1-3

[2] "History of the JDA." <u>Village News.</u> September 26, 2012: pg. 6

Bibliography

The primary sources used for background information on the history and development of motels were <u>The Motel in America</u> by John A. Jakle, Keith A. Schulle, and Jefferson S. Rogers, published in 1996, and <u>America on the Road: From Autocamp to Motel, 1910-1945</u> by Warren-James Belasco, published in 1979. Both works remain the primary sources for the social history of motels as well as their business history.

A variety of motel guides from the author's collection published from the 1920's to the 1950's provided detailed descriptions of motels and tourist homes in the area. They include guides published by Quality Courts, Superior Courts, American Motel Association, and the 1950 and 1960 editions of the Virginia Tourist Court Guide. These descriptions contain the amenities each motel offered and provide great insight as to what motel owners offered over the years to meet the public's evolving expectations.

Newspaper sources provided local history articles and 1930's and '40's articles from the <u>Richmond News Leader</u>, revealed official concerns about road side camps and their corrupting influences. The Chester <u>Village News</u> was a source for articles and interviews about early travel and accommodations along Highway 1 in Chesterfield County.

Government documents obtained online from the Department of Agriculture, the Federal Highway Administration, and the Virginia Department of Transportation were the source of historical road-building information and U.S. Highway 1 history. A number of related articles were found online, with topics ranging from postcard history to general motel history.

A primary objective of this project was to track down motels no longer in existence and to determine where they were located and when they were built. To find locations, roadside searches were conducted as well as virtual searches using Google Earth. This online resource was invaluable in obtaining aerial views that provided hints of motel locations both current and historical. In addition, historical aerial photographs, along with vintage topographical maps available online from the U.S. Geological Survey provided additional clues. Other valuable online resources included the Geographical Information Services (GIS) of Henrico, Richmond City, and Chesterfield counties which often provided information on the year a motel was built along with its current street address.

Research was conducted at the Chesterfield County Library, Chesterfield County Historical Society, Virginia State Library, Virginia Department of Historic Resources, the Chesterfield County Circuit Court Clerk Records Branch, and the Chesterfield County Department of Real Estate Assessment. Mr. David Malgee, local historian, provided information on locations of motels no longer standing. Mike Uzel provided postcards from his collection to supplement those in the narrative and provided invaluable assistance with local history.

Books and Booklets:

Associated Tour Guide, 1928. New York. The Automobile Club of America. 1928.

Belasco, Warren James. America on the Road: From Autocamp to Motel, 1910-1945. Baltimore and London: The Johns Hopkins University Press, 1979.

Federal Hi-Way Silent-Nite Homes. Minneapolis: Federal Hi-Way Silent-Nite Homes, 1939.

Hines, Duncan. Lodging for the Night. Bowling Green: Adventures in Good Eating, Inc., 1946.

Jakle, John A., et al. The Motel in America. Baltimore and London: The Johns Hopkins University Press, 1996.

Margolies, John. Home Away From Home; Motels in America. Boston, New York, Toronto, London: Little, Brown, and Company, 1995.

The Negro Motorist Green Book. New York. Victor H. Green. 1949.

O'Dell, Jeffrey M. Chesterfield County Early Architecture and Historic Sites. Chesterfield County: Chesterfield County, Virginia, 1983.

Virginia State. Virginia Department of Transportation. History of Roads in Virginia: "The Most Convenient Wayes". Richmond: Commonwealth of Virginia, 2006.

Witzel, Michael Karl. The American Motel. Osceola: MBI Publishing Company, 2000.

Wood, Andrew F., and Jenny L. Wood. Motel in America. Portland: Collectors Press, 2004.

Pamphlets & Brochures

American Motel Association Guide. Ridgewood, NJ: American Motel Association, 1958.

American Motel Association Guide. Newark, NJ: American Motel Association, 1951.

Eastern States Maine to Florida 1952-53 Mutual Travel Index. Boston, MA: Mutual Travel Index, 1952.

Finest Tourist Homes, De-Luxe Cottage Courts, Excellent Restaurants. East Orange, NJ: American Motel Association, 1940.

National Motor Travel Guide. Denver, CO: United Motor Courts, Inc., 1948.

McRorie's Tourist Guide. Jacksonville, FL: McRorie's Tourist Home, 1935.

Motel Guide to Happy Motoring. Newark, NJ: American Motel Association, 1949.

Quality Courts United Guide 1950-51. Quality Courts United Inc., 1950.

Quality Courts United Guide, 1958. Quality Courts United Inc., 1958

Quality Courts United Guide, Revised 1945. Quality Courts United Inc., 1945.

Superior Courts United Guide, 1958. Superior Courts United, Inc., 1958.

United Motor Courts Guide. 1937.

Virginia Tourist Court Guide. Virginia: Virginia Tourist Court Association, 1950.

Your National Motor Travel Guide. Denver, CO: United Motor Courts, Inc., 1950.

Newspaper Articles:

Chesterfield Plus. October 3, 1990.

"Former Jeff Davis motel is home to several businesses". Village News. January 28, 2009: pg. 11

"History of the JDA." Village News. September 26, 2012: pg. 6

"Interview with Otha Lee Taylor – Reminiscence – Life on the Pike." Village News. July 28, 2010.

"Remember When: Shady Side and Sunny Side Once Popular Stopovers for Tourists". Village News. 3 Sep. 2008: pg. 12

The Richmond News Leader.

"Police Check Tourist Camps in County". 11 Jul. 1940: pg. 2
" 'Different' Road Camps". 31 May 1938: pg. 10
"Tourist Homes, After Early Knockout, Come Up Fighting". 11 Aug. 1942: pg. 3
"Conditions At Road Camps". 21 Dec. 1939: pg. 10
"Tourist Camp Definition Stumps Legislative Group". 2 Feb. 1940: pg 1
"Tourist Camp Bill To Cut Teeth In June". 21 Mar. 1940: pg. 5
"State Operators of Tourist Courts and Home Organize". 16 Jun. 1941: pg. 15
"Finds Tourist Camps Often Put to Immoral Use". 21 Dec. 1939: pgs. 1-2
"Hotel Boom Unprecedented, Observers Say". 20 Apr. 1984: pgs 1-3

Unpublished Manuscripts:

Ridout, John. "A History of the Route 1 Corridor". Chesterfield County Office of Revitalization, July 2006

Wells, John E. "Brief Context for Motels and Motor Courts, Rt. 1, Central Virginia, VDOT – Richmond District". 11 Jul 2006

Online Sources:

"The Atlantic Highway". 15 May 2012.
<http://en.wikipedia.org/wiki/Atlantic_Highway_%28United_States%29#History>

"Camps of Crime". American Magazine. February 1940. 12 July 2012.
<http://en.wikipedia.org/wiki/Motel>

" Chamberlayne Avenue ;Brief illustrated history of Chamberlayne Avenue as a tourist stopover on historic US Route 1". 26 September 2012. <http://chamberlayneave.blogspot.com/>

"The Guide That Helped Black Motorists Drive Around Jim Crow". 12 August 2012.
<http://jalopnik.com/5735788/the-guide-that-helped-black-motorists-drive-around-jim-crow!date=>

Kozel, Scott M. "Richmond Interstates and Expressways". 30 July 2007.
<http://www.roadstothefuture.com/Richmond_Interstate_Expy.html>

---. "Richmond-Petersburg Turnpike". 25 April 2012.
<http://www.roadstothefuture.com/Richmond_Interstate_Expy.html#RP_Tpk>

McGee, Celia. "The Open Road Wasn't Quite Open to All". 12 August 2012.
<http://www.nytimes.com/2010/08/23/books/23green.html?_r=1>

"Motel". 3 August 2012. < http://en.wikipedia.org/wiki/Motel>

"Postcard Collecting History". 18 August 2012. < http://www.postcardy.com/collecting.html>

"Transportation Indicators for Motor Vehicles and Airlines: 1900-2001". 25 June 2012.
<http://www.census.gov/statab/hist/HS-41.pdf>

United States. U. S. Department of Agriculture. United States Route No. 1 is a Highway of History. 9 Oct. 1927. 25 April 2012. <http://www.fhwa.dot.gov/highwayhistory/us1pr.cfm>

United States. Federal Highway Administration. "U.S. 1: Fort Kent, Maine to Key West, Florida". nd. 25 April 2012. <http://www.fhwa.dot.gov/highwayhistory/us1.cfm>

"Virginia Highways Page US Routes 1 and Branches". 22 July 2007.
<http://www.angelfire.com/va3/mapmikey/US1.html>

"Virginia Historical Highway Markers Search, Electric Railway". 3 October 2012.
<http://www.dhr.virginia.gov/hiway_markers/marker.cfm?mid=2298>

Weingroff, Richard F. "Vol. I, No. 1 - The First Issue of Public Roads, May 1918". 5 March 2012.
<http://www.fhwa.dot.gov/publications/publicroads/00mayjun/volume1.cfm>

---. "From Names to Numbers: The Origins of the U.S. Numbered Highway System". 25 April 2012. < http://www.fhwa.dot.gov/infrastructure/numbers.cfm>

---. "Jefferson Davis Memorial Highway". 25 April 2012. <http://www.fhwa.dot.gov/infrastructure/jdavis.cfm>

Maps & Photographs:

The following maps and aerial photographs were obtained online from <http://www.usgs.gov/> from 26-28 May 2012

"Bermuda Hundred VA". Map. 1946.
"Chester VA". Map. 1952.
"Chester VA". Map. 1944.
"Drewry's Bluff VA". Map. 1938.
"Drewry's Bluff VA". Map. 1952.
"Petersburg VA". Map. 1969.
"Petersburg VA". Map. 1944.
"Richmond VA". Map. 1934.
"Richmond VA". Map. 1956.
"Richmond VA". Map. 1964.
"Richmond VA". Map. 1939.
"Chester VA". Aerial Photographs. 1968.
"Chesterfield VA". Aerial Photographs. 1968.
"Colonial Heights VA". Aerial Photographs. 1968.
"Petersburg VA". Aerial Photographs. 1968.

Virginia. "Official State Highway Map, 1941-1942". Virginia Department of Highways.

Virginia. "Richmond Petersburg Turnpike". Richmond-Petersburg Turnpike Authority. nd.